Mountains

Kenna Bourke

Series editor **Sue Palmer**

OXFORD
UNIVERSITY PRESS

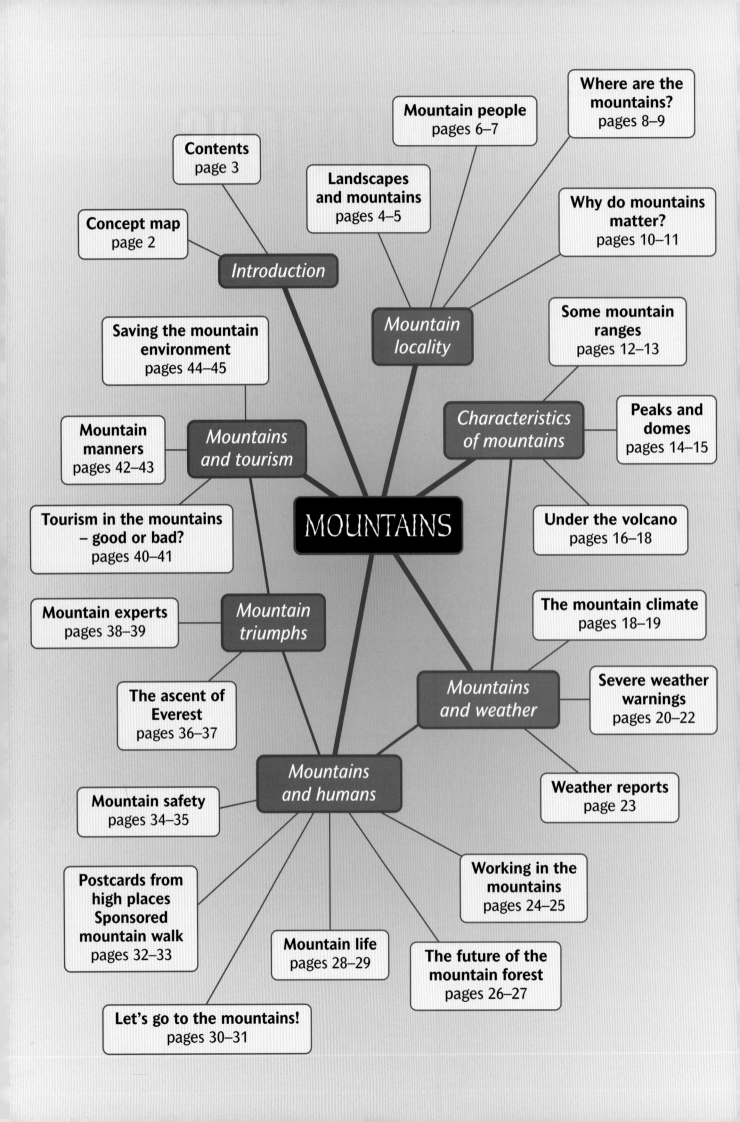

MOUNTAINS

Introduction
- Concept map — page 2
- Contents — page 3

Mountain locality
- Landscapes and mountains — pages 4–5
- Mountain people — pages 6–7
- Where are the mountains? — pages 8–9
- Why do mountains matter? — pages 10–11

Characteristics of mountains
- Some mountain ranges — pages 12–13
- Peaks and domes — pages 14–15
- Under the volcano — pages 16–18

Mountains and weather
- The mountain climate — pages 18–19
- Severe weather warnings — pages 20–22
- Weather reports — page 23

Mountains and humans
- Working in the mountains — pages 24–25
- The future of the mountain forest — pages 26–27
- Mountain life — pages 28–29
- Let's go to the mountains! — pages 30–31
- Postcards from high places Sponsored mountain walk — pages 32–33
- Mountain safety — pages 34–35

Mountain triumphs
- The ascent of Everest — pages 36–37
- Mountain experts — pages 38–39

Mountains and tourism
- Tourism in the mountains – good or bad? — pages 40–41
- Mountain manners — pages 42–43
- Saving the mountain environment — pages 44–45

Contents

Mountains shape the Earth we live on and the life-style of the people who live in them. My favourite pages are about mountain people because it is amazing to find out how they survive in such harsh conditions. I also liked reading the pages about how we are destroying the mountain environment and how we can protect it.

Tashi Sherpa
Kathmandu, Nepal
(age 10)

Landscapes and mountains

- Deserts cover a third of the world's land surface. They are found in North and South America, Africa, Asia and Australia.

- The largest desert is the Sahara.

- Mountains cover about a quarter of our planet's land surface.

- The world's highest mountain is Everest (8853 m).

- Forests cover about 30% of the Earth's land.

- There are three main types of forest: **broadleaf**, **coniferous** and **rainforest**.

Is it a hill or a mountain?

Surprisingly enough, no one can agree on the difference between a hill and a mountain. However, it is true to say that a mountain usually has a peak or summit that you can see. In Britain, a hill becomes a mountain when it is over 600 metres, or over 300 metres if it looks substantially different from the countryside surrounding it.

The highest peak in the UK is Ben Nevis, in the Grampian Mountains in Scotland. It is 1344 metres high. A close second is Snowdon in the Cambrian Mountains in Wales, at 1085 metres.

- Oceans and seas cover 71% of the surface of our planet.

- The biggest is the Pacific Ocean, which covers a third of the surface of the world.

Mountain people

A tenth of the world's total population lives in the mountains. Mountains are home to several thousand different **tribes** or ethnic groups.

The Sherpas of Nepal

The word 'Sherpa' means 'people of the east'. Sherpa people originally came from eastern Tibet, but from about AD 1400 onwards, this mountain tribe began to migrate, and today about 36,000 Sherpas live in the Himalayas, in Nepal. No one on Earth lives at a higher **altitude** than the Sherpas.

The Sherpas are very well equipped for mountain living. They have lived for centuries at high altitude, and so their lungs have developed more fully than those of people who live at lower altitudes. Therefore, they are able to pump oxygen into their bloodstream and muscles much more efficiently than many other people. This, combined with the fact that they are generally small and stocky, helps them to

tolerate low temperatures, and enables them to climb very high mountains. As a result they have acquired an international reputation as first class mountain guides. When, in 1953, Sir Edmund Hillary made the first successful attempt at climbing Mount Everest, his guide was a Sherpa called Tenzing Norgay.

The Sherpas were trading people, and still are to this day. Many retain their traditional customs, raising yaks for wool and leather, as well as milk, butter and cheese. They also grow potatoes, barley and maize, which provide them with food. A traditional Sherpa dish is 'shyakpa' – a kind of yak meat and potato stew.

A Sherpa carrying a heavy load

Harvesting potatoes in Bolivia

The Andean people

The Andes is the longest mountain **range** in the world. It extends over seven countries in South America, from Venezuela in the north to Argentina in the south.

The people living there are descended from the Incas, a powerful people who built one of the richest and biggest empires in the **western hemisphere**. It extended over 4000 kilometres and had the city of Cusco in southern Peru as its capital. The Andes are rich in **minerals**, including gold, silver, tin and copper. In the sixteenth century, the Spanish conquered the area in order to profit from the gold and silver.

Today, **mining** is still one of the major human activities in the region, along with farming. Grain and potatoes are grown and sheep, llamas and alpacas are bred for their wool. Tourism is also important, with large numbers of people visiting the old Inca sites of Machu Picchu and Cusco.

The hill tribes of Mount Kinabalu

On Sabah, an island in Malaysia, stands Mount Kinabalu. At 4101 metres, it is the highest peak in the Malay **archipelago**. The slopes of Kinabalu are the home of hill tribes, including the Dusuns and the Kadazans, to whom the mountain is sacred. They believe that Mount Kinabalu is the resting place of the souls of the dead. 'Kinabalu' means 'dwelling place of the dead'.

Children from the Dusun tribe performing the Harvest Dance

Where are the mountains?

There are many mountain **ranges** in the world. Here are six of them. However, some of the highest mountains are not part of ranges.

A

Highest peak in North America:
Mount McKinley, Alaska, 6194 m

Mount McKinley

Rocky Mountains

NORTH
AMERICA

Appalachians

Mountain range: The Alps

Total length: 1200 km

Highest peak:
Mont Blanc, 4807 m

NORTH
ATLANTIC
OCEAN

Mont Blanc

Mountain range:
Rocky Mountains

Total length: 3220 km

Highest Peak:
Mount Elbert, 4399 m

Mount Elbert

Mount Mitchell

Mountain range: Appalachians

Total length: 2400 km

Highest peak: Mount Mitchell, 2037 m

PACIFIC
OCEAN

SOUTH
AMERICA

Andes

Mountain range:
The Andes

Total length: 8000 km

Highest peak: Cerro
Aconcagua, 6959 m

Cerro Aconcagua

SOUTH
ATLANTIC
OCEAN

SOUTHERN OCEAN

Highest peak in Antarctica:
Vinson Massif, 5140 m

Vinson Massif

OCEAN

Mountain range: The Urals

Total length: 2400 km

Highest peak: Gora Narodnaya, 1895 m

Arctic Circle

▲ Gora Narodnaya

U
r
a
l
s

ASIA

EUROPE

▲ Elbrus

Himalayas

Mountain range: The Himalayas

Total length: 2400 km

Highest peak: Everest, 8848 m

PACIFIC
OCEAN

Highest peak
in Europe:
Elbrus, 5642 m

▲ Everest

Tropic of Cancer

RICA

Equator

▲ Kilimanjaro

INDIAN
OCEAN

Highest peak in Africa:
Kilimanjaro, 5895 m

Tropic of Capricorn

OCEANIA

Mount Cook
▲

Highest peak in Oceania:
Mount Cook, 3754 m

SOUTHERN OCEAN

Antarctic Circle

ANTARCTICA

Why do mountains matter?

Water

One very important reason why mountains matter is that they provide fresh water for over half the people of the world. Mountains are sometimes described as the 'water towers' of the world. Most of this water is stored as snow and **glaciers** and released in rivers, waterfalls and streams. All the world's big rivers have their **headwaters** in mountains. The Rio Grande, for example, takes 80% of its water from the Rocky Mountains. The size and shape of a mountain forces air upwards, where it condenses (small water droplets are formed) to make clouds. When the droplets of water become too heavy, they fall as rain or snow.

Food and plants

Another reason that mountains matter to our planet is that 20 types of plant supply 80% of the world's food, and six of these plants originally came from the mountains. The potato, which can withstand extreme frosts, first grew in the Andes. Today, farmers in the Andes know of up to 2000 different species of potato. In the mountains of Nepal, about 2000 different types of rice are farmed. In the Mexican Sierra Mountains, the very first corn was found growing.

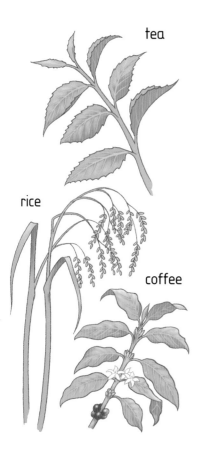

tea

rice

coffee

The best quality teas and coffees are grown at around 1500 m. Because many mountain regions are difficult to reach, lots of species of plant have been preserved from **plunder** by humans.

Potatoes for sale in a market in Peru

Animals

Mountains also matter because they are home to many animals that are found nowhere else on Earth. Mountain gorillas in the Ruwenzori Mountains of East Africa; spectacled bears in the Andes; and quetzals in Central America are among those becoming increasingly rare. As an example of the variety of wildlife a mountain can sustain, Mount Cameroon, the highest mountain in West Africa, has 210 bird species and 70 butterfly species. Without mountains, therefore, the **fauna** and **flora** of our planet would be much poorer.

A quetzal

A mountain gorilla

Some mountain ranges

The Rocky Mountains: North America

- Chain of rugged mountains stretching from New Mexico to British Columbia
- Very steep slopes
- Jagged, snow-capped peaks
- Numerous **glaciers**
- Many rivers and lakes
- Few inhabitants

The Himalayas: Nepal, China and Tibet

- World's highest mountain system
- Contains nine of the world's ten highest peaks
- Inhabited by nearly 40 million people
- Climate ranges from **subtropical** in southern foothills (temperatures in summer reaching 30°C) to −20°C at highest points

Mountain ranges

Grampian Mountains: Scotland

- Ranging from gentle slopes to rugged peaks
- Highest peak, Ben Nevis (1344 m)
- Low temperatures and heavy snowfalls common in winter
- Few inhabitants

The mountains of the Sinai desert: Egypt

This is a jagged system of mountains and **wadis**, the highest peak of which is Mount Catherine, 2637 m. The climate is hot and dry, with less than 4 mm of rain a year. Mount Sinai, 2285 metres, is the sacred mountain on which, according to the Old Testament, Moses received the Ten Commandments. Bedouin tribes live in the area.

The Alps: France, Italy, Switzerland and Germany

- Highest and most inhabited mountains in Europe
- Inhabited by approximately 20 million people
- 2% of the Alps covered in ice
- Longest glacier: the Aletsch glacier (18 km long)
- Rainfall on northern side up to 3000 mm a year
- Pine forests on lower slopes
- Perpetually snow-capped peaks

Peaks and domes

Different kinds of mountain are formed in different ways. There are four types: fold, fault, dome and volcano. Most mountains were formed many millions of years ago and since their formation, erosion has played a major part in making them look like they do today.

The most common type of mountain is the fold mountain.

Fold mountains

The Earth's crust is divided into large sections called plates. The plates are huge chunks of rock that float on the top of the soft **mantle** of the Earth. **Geologists** believe that the Earth's plates are constantly moving at a speed of about 1–10 cm a year. Sometimes two plates crash into each other. When they collide, they create intense pressure, causing the plates to buckle. This causes rock to be pushed upwards, forming a mountain. Imagine taking a piece of paper and putting it flat on your desk. If you pushed the two ends towards each other, you would get an upward fold in the middle. That's what can happen when the Earth's plates collide with each other.

A good example of a chain of fold mountains is the Himalayas. They were created 25 million years ago because the Indian plate collided with the Eurasian plate. An older chain of fold mountains is the Urals. They are approximately 200 million years old.

Fault block mountains

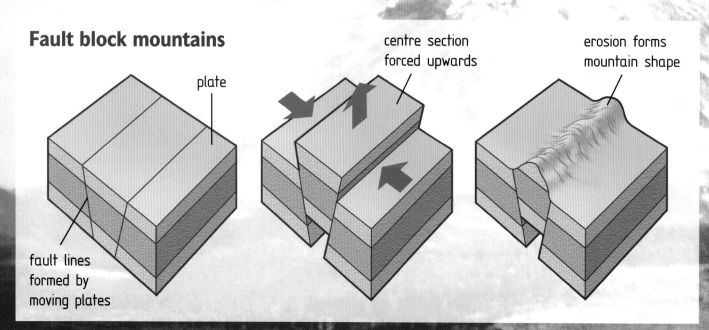

plate

centre section forced upwards

erosion forms mountain shape

fault lines formed by moving plates

Dome mountains

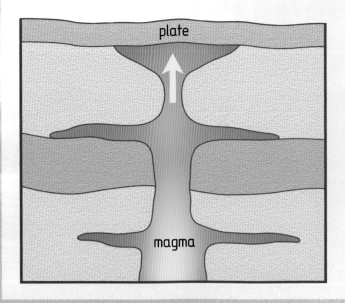
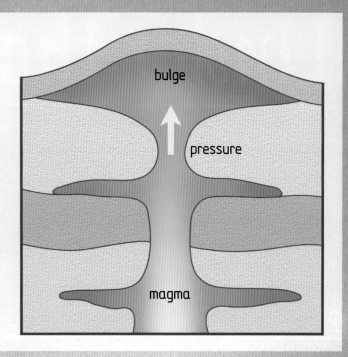

How a volcano is formed

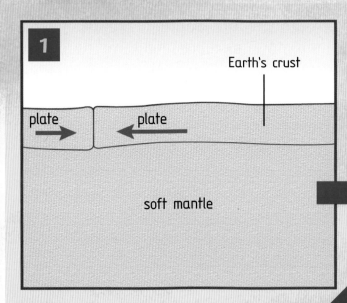

1

Earth's crust

plate → ← plate

soft mantle

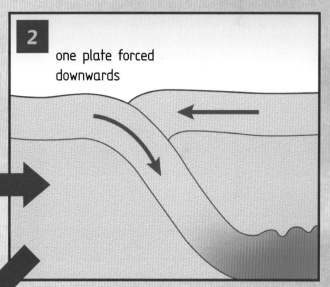

2

one plate forced downwards

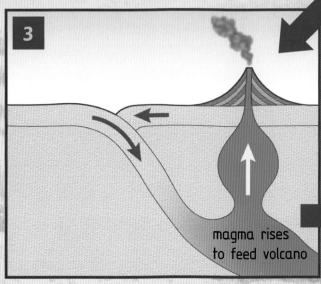

3

magma rises to feed volcano

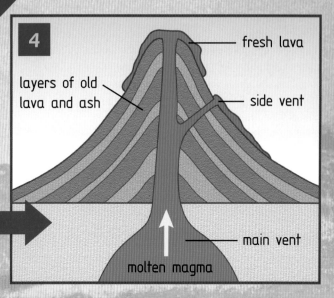

4

fresh lava

layers of old lava and ash

side vent

main vent

molten magma

Under the volcano

Why do people live in volcanic areas?

Electricity

In some parts of the world, steam from volcanic activity is used to make electricity or used to heat homes. The big advantage of this energy is that it is very clean and the resources are likely to last for a very long time. New Zealand and Iceland are two countries which use this natural energy source.

Minerals

When a volcano erupts, it throws out a large amount of ash. At the time of the eruption, the ash can be harmful to the environment but as it cools it forms a layer on the surface. The ash layer is full of useful **minerals** which help to make the soil fertile and easy to farm, so that the local farmers can grow healthy crops.

Magma can be mined once it has cooled on the surface as lava. It can contain gold, silver, as well as diamonds, copper and zinc, and as a result bring wealth to the area.

Water

Like other mountains, volcanoes act as water reservoirs, providing the people who live nearby with fresh water. Hot **springs** are also often found in volcanic sites.

Tourism

Often volcanoes and volcanic areas are very beautiful, and attract many tourists. Because of the tourist industry local people are able to get jobs in shops, restaurants and cafés. The volcanic islands of Hawaii benefit greatly from tourism.

A hot spring in Iceland next to a power plant producing **geothermal energy**

Reasons not to live in volcanic areas

Over the centuries volcanoes have killed thousands of people and destroyed towns and villages. Many volcanoes are still active. That is to say that they could and probably will erupt again. Popocatepetl is a volcano in Mexico, 50 km from the capital, Mexico City. Its name comes from the Native American Nahuatl language and means 'smoking mountain'. **Vulcanologists** consider Popocatepetl to be one of the most dangerous volcanoes in the world. It has erupted over 20 times since 1354. Its last major eruption was in 1947 but it has thrown out gas and ash as recently as 1998, covering the surrounding valley. Over 30,000 people had to be evacuated.

The volcano Popocatepe erupting in 199

What to do if a volcano erupts

BEFORE

A Make **evacuation** plans

Escape route	Emergency communication plan	Meeting points and contact numbers

B Make sure you have your kit

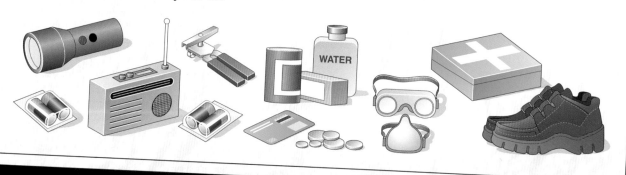

DURING

If caught near home

Follow evacuation order	CLOSE !	CLOSE !	CLOSE !

If caught away from home

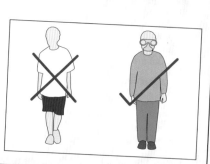

AFTER

STAY AWAY
ASH FALL

The mountain climate

The mountain climate varies depending on where in the world the mountain is. The lower reaches of Mount Kilimanjaro in Tanzania, Africa, are warmer than the lower reaches of the Alps. However, for all mountains the higher up you go, the colder it gets.

Mountain climate	Plants	Animals	Weather conditions
Peak	No **vegetation**	No animals	Extreme cold, **blizzards**, **avalanches**, snow all year round
Higher slopes	Small, low-lying plants, alpine flowers, lichens, mosses, etc.	Few, hardy species: mountain goats, chamois, llamas, yak, takin, snow leopard, ibex, etc.	Cold, wet and windy, snow in winter
Lower slopes	Forests of **evergreen** and **deciduous** trees	Many species of animal	Warm, maybe some snow in winter

Squirrel

Blizzards

Ibex

Alpine flowers

Evergreen and deciduous forests

Severe weather warnings

The Daily News

Friday 26th February, 1999

Three Men Survive Blizzard

By Paul Webster in Paris

"They dug into a drift on the mountain and closed the hole behind them. It was like a marmot's den."

Three Alpine skiers who spent nine nights at 3000 metres in **blizzards** and sub-zero temperatures were recovering in hospital yesterday after a rescue operation that combined raw courage, ingenuity and high technology. A week after they lost their way in a blizzard while trekking across peaks in the Savoie, France, the three were saved after France Telecoms pinpointed a call on their portable telephone. The rescue team leader said the 'excellent' survival techniques used by the three men, who built an igloo inside a 10-metre-high snowdrift, should be used as an example for all mountaineers.

Landslides, Kumaon Hills, Himalayas, India – August 1998

11th August

*Rocks and mud **cascaded** 7 km down mountain slopes into Kali river.*

*River burst banks. Wall of mud, rock and water barrelled down the **gorge**.*

70 people killed.

12th August

*Rescue teams recover 31 bodies from **debris**. 39 others remain untraced.*

No human habitation left as more villages washed away.

The men set off for a four-day ski trek on Monday 15 February. Five days after they had set off, the men made their first call to rescuers. They could give no accurate information on where they were holed up.

The leader of the mountain rescue team, Gérard Valich, a police captain, said:

"They called again twice on Sunday but the battery ran out before the call could be traced."

Captain Valich reports, "We thought we had lost touch but they were able to make a brief call on Tuesday. Later we realized that rescue teams on foot had passed close to the igloo and that the men had even heard whistles."

The 100-strong rescue team was hampered by snowstorms and 120 kph winds which prevented helicopter crews from searching the slopes.

However, yesterday, despite their ordeal, the three men walked from rescue helicopters which had spotted them as one of the men prepared to risk avalanches and ski down the mountain for help.

While the men were receiving treatment for slight frostbite at Moutiers hospital, Captain Valich said the igloo shelter had been so effective that the interior was almost snug. "They dug into a drift on the mountain wall and then closed the hole behind them," he said. "It was like a marmot's den. The temperature was about two degrees Celsius inside and minus twenty outside. Each time they climbed out to make a telephone call the temperature inside dropped terribly, so they preferred to dig themselves in and wait for better weather."

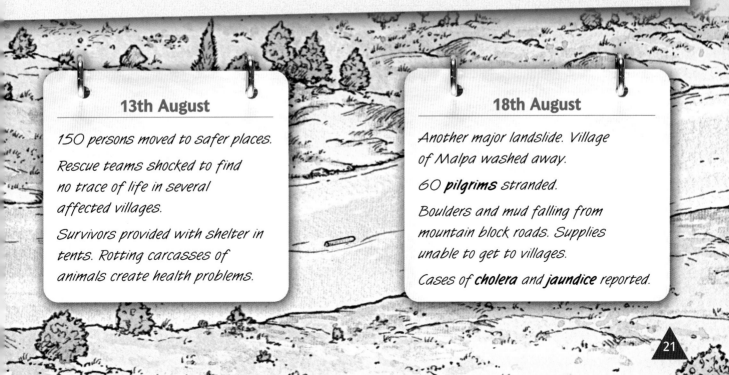

13th August

150 persons moved to safer places.

Rescue teams shocked to find no trace of life in several affected villages.

Survivors provided with shelter in tents. Rotting carcasses of animals create health problems.

18th August

Another major landslide. Village of Malpa washed away.

60 **pilgrims** stranded.

Boulders and mud falling from mountain block roads. Supplies unable to get to villages.

Cases of **cholera** and **jaundice** reported.

Avalanche

Tuesday 6 February

Arrived at hotel in Haute Savoie. Snow falling heavily. We hope we will be able to do some skiing tomorrow. Others in hotel say snow has been falling for three days.

Wednesday 7 February

Woke up to clear skies. Got our skis on and set off up the mountain. Very beautiful! Sadly, early afternoon, the beauty was shattered by a terrible sight. A huge cloud of tumbling snow was seen speeding down the mountain just 1 km or less from where we stood. A huge roar filled the valley. People stopped in their tracks and stared. A murmur of 'avalanche' could be heard on everybody's lips.

Returned to hotel with heavy hearts.

Thursday 8 February

The hotel was buzzing with news of the disaster. By the end of the day, all we knew was that 10 people had died – three women, three men and four children. A rescue party of 200 had been scouring the slopes all day for signs of life and 27 people had been rescued from the snow. One person was in hospital with hypothermia.

Friday 9 February

We have been evacuated to a safer resort in case of further avalanches. Even though our village wasn't hit by the avalanche, in neighbouring villages a total of 23 chalets have been destroyed. It was difficult getting to our new hotel, as many of the roads were blocked by snow and the coach had to wait for snowploughs. In the end we found a different route.

Saturday 10 February

We heard this morning that two people are still missing. What horror for their families. Will we ever get home? The Mont Blanc tunnel has been closed and there are no train services.

Weather reports

Daytime temperature in the Andes

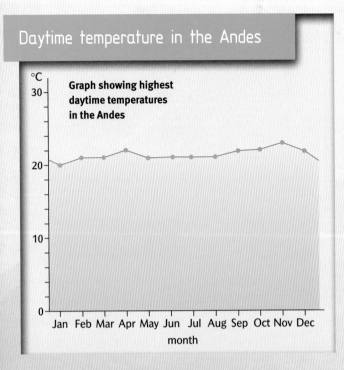

In the Andes, the temperature does not vary that much over the year, being slightly colder in the winter months from May to September.

Daytime temperature in the Alps

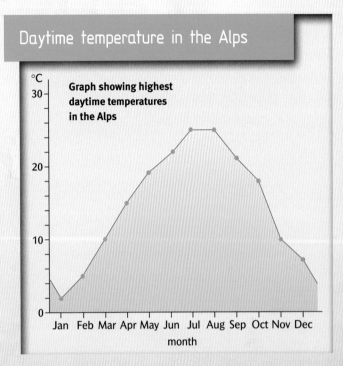

In the Alps, the temperature varies a lot more between winter and summer. In winter the temperature can be as low as 2°C and in summer as high as 25°C.

Rainfall in Alps

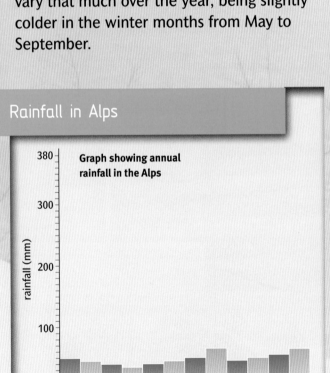

Rainfall in Himalayas

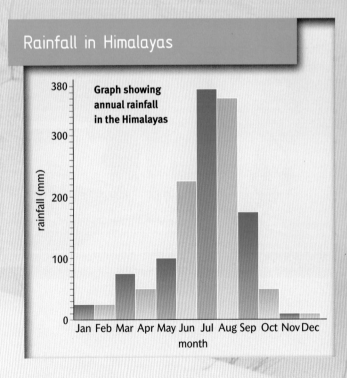

Working in the mountains

Mountain areas support a variety of industries from traditional farming and crafts to mining, energy production, forestry and tourism. The mountain climate plays an important part in the type of industry that exists.

wood products — logging — **forestry**

paper

hydro-electric power — **energy production**

How the weather influences working in mountains

Snow

ski instructors — **skiing**

tourism

hotels and restaurants

Rainfall

rice

tea

farming

crops

strawberries

animals

potatoes

meat, milk, etc

carpets

wool,
e.g. cashmere

The future of the mountain forest

Healthy mountain forests are extremely important to the world. They protect the **watersheds** that supply half the fresh water we use. They are also home to thousands of species of wild animals and plants. At the same time, the wood that they provide gives many thousands of people a source of money. Should we protect the forests or should we allow them to be cut down?

There are two ways of looking at the future of forests. On the one hand people say that forests are renewable: trees that are cut down can be replaced with new ones. On the other hand, **conservationists** believe that cutting down forests may have very dangerous consequences for all of us.

Deforestation in Oregon, USA

The people who see forests as a renewable resource argue that we need the wood that forests provide for timber products and paper products. Many poor communities around the world depend on forests for their livelihood. If they are no longer allowed to cut trees down, they will have to find other ways of earning a living. That might mean that they are forced to move out of the mountain areas to big cities to live in slums, away from their families. It is therefore important that mountain communities are maintained.

The chinchilla – hunted to near extinction in the wild

Philippine village affected by flood damage

The tahr – endangered in the wild

In response to these arguments, conservationists point out that large areas of rainforest and forest are disappearing daily, destroying rare plants, and endangering animals. Once these are gone, we can't replace them. Furthermore, as forests are cut down, river beds begin to dry up because there is less rain without the trees. This threatens more species and the one thing every person in the world needs to survive: water. As if that were not enough, the more forests are cut down, the greater the risk of natural disasters such as avalanches, landslides and floods; disasters which kill many people every year.

Therefore, it seems that although there are many arguments in favour of cutting down mountain forests, we should think very carefully before allowing a wide-scale logging programme to continue. Perhaps the answer is that we should limit the amount of logging that is allowed each year in an effort to maintain a balance between the immediate needs of the people and the needs of nature.

Mountain life

The mountains are beautiful to look at.

We can go skiing and sledging without having to travel far.

The air is clean and healthy.

There are lots of things to do like snowboarding, going for walks, and having snowball fights!

You keep fit because you're always walking up or down a hill.

There are lots of animals and plants that you'd never see if you lived in a city.

You meet lots of new people because it's a tourist area.

There's lots of work during the tourist season.

Teenagers can get part-time jobs too.

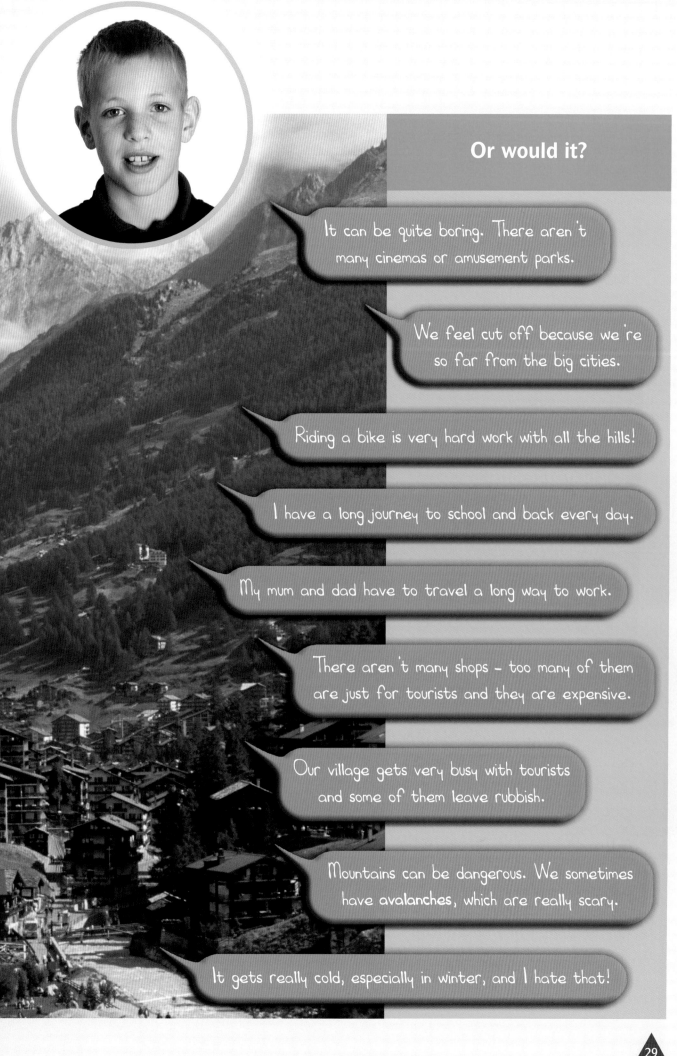

Or would it?

It can be quite boring. There aren't many cinemas or amusement parks.

We feel cut off because we're so far from the big cities.

Riding a bike is very hard work with all the hills!

I have a long journey to school and back every day.

My mum and dad have to travel a long way to work.

There aren't many shops – too many of them are just for tourists and they are expensive.

Our village gets very busy with tourists and some of them leave rubbish.

Mountains can be dangerous. We sometimes have avalanches, which are really scary.

It gets really cold, especially in winter, and I hate that!

Let's go to the mountains!

Escape the pressures of modern-day life with a holiday in the

BEAUTIFUL MOUNTAINS!

Chamonix, one of Europe's most celebrated resorts, dominated by the legendary snow-capped Mont Blanc.

Chamonix is famed for its spectacular setting with views up to Mont Blanc, the Aiguille du Midi and the shimmering Glacier des Bossons. On the other side of the valley are the reddish jagged peaks of the Aiguilles Rouges. This is a resort with much to offer the summer visitor.

A trip on the cable car up to the Aiguille du Midi is a must, offering spectacular, panoramic views of the French, Italian and Swiss Alps. Discover the area's natural beauty with a ride on the cog railway to the 'Mer de Glace' **glacier** or a visit to the Aiguilles Rouges nature reserve. There is a great range of activities on offer and the town, with its lovely flower-lined streets, has a wealth of shops to browse. You'll also find numerous cafés, tempting restaurants and lively nightspots.

Just 6 km further up the valley lies the delightful village of Argentière, dominated by the stunning terrain of the Grands Montets glacier. Walkers will enjoy the option to explore the valley from their doorstep, via the Grands Montets cable car or by the efficient local bus service. In the evening relax with a drink or meal in one of the village bars or restaurants.

Three Peaks Explorer Holiday

Climb the highest mountains of Scotland, Wales and England!

See castles, glens and villages.

Sail Lake Windermere

Informative and experienced guides

- Carefully chosen **itineraries**
- Everything from transportation to accommodation
- Full cooked breakfasts, sumptuous lunches, first class dinners!
- Areas of outstanding natural beauty
- Magnificent panoramas, stunning scenery
- Learn about history and culture
- Small groups, personal attention
- Friendly, relaxed atmosphere

Postcards from high places

---

2 August 03

Dear Nick

Here I am in Sutherland, in Scotland. Today I climbed to the top of Suilven! It's not particularly high (731 m) but it's a fantastic mountain to climb.

It's shaped a bit like a policeman's helmet! Apparently its name is from an old Norse word that means 'pillar mountain'.

The Vikings must have been able to see it from the sea as they approached the coast of Scotland. The view from the top is awesome – just miles and miles of wilderness! You really must see it one day.

Jack

Nick Feather

201 Drove Lane

Cupplestone

CP32 7YU

January 2003

Dear Mum and Dad

I've done it! Last night Tony and I climbed Mount Sinai to see the sun rise. It was the most incredible sight you can imagine – just like looking at a sea of red rock for miles around. We started off at midnight with a Bedouin guide to help us stay on the right track. The climb at first is quite gentle but the further up you go, the harder it gets. After about two hours we came to a little stall selling hot minty tea, which was delicious, and just what we needed because it gets very cold in the desert at night. We set off again and finally reached the summit at 4.45 am. There's a tiny church at the top but not much else. Then the sun began to rise and everyone went very quiet and just watched in amazement as the huge red disk peeped up in the distance. I wish you'd been there to see it!

Lots of love

Isabelle

Taylor Family
6 Acre Street
Runsworth
RW16 8DV

Monday 3 February

Hi everyone!

The snow here is great. We've been out skiing all day and I fell over about a hundred times but it was brilliant. We went up the mountain on a chair lift, which is a bit scary if you look down at the ground but very exciting too. Keith says that they ought to cut down some of the trees because they're in the way but I reckon that's just because he's not very good at skiing yet. He crashed into one very spectacularly but didn't seem to find it as funny as I did!

Bye for now!

James

Sponsored mountain walk

Mount Pleasant
Newtown
Hopeshire
HH4 8BP

29 October 2002

Dear Uncle Freddy, Aunty Eloise and Oscar

I'm writing to ask if you will sponsor me. I'm going to do a mountain walk for charity. The charity I've chosen is the Leprosy Mission. Let me tell you a bit about it.

Leprosy is a disease which affects millions of people all over the world. A lot of people who haven't got it are very frightened of leprosy because they think it's easy to catch but it isn't! They're also scared because leprosy can cause blindness and it can paralyse your hands, feet and face if it's left untreated. What that really means is that the people who do have it are often quite badly treated by people who don't. The really fantastic thing is that leprosy is curable! The Leprosy Mission helps these people who are suffering from leprosy by providing them with a drug called MDT. So far more than ten million people have been cured with this drug. That's why I want to help.

The walk I'm going to do is in the Brecon Beacons, in Wales. A group of us will walk 42 km in the shortest time we can. If you think that I can do it, and you want to help people with leprosy, please sponsor me! You can either sponsor me for every kilometre I walk, or if you prefer, you can just put a total amount. Any amount will do! Even 50p will help. Thanks very much!

Best wishes

Jonathan

EXPEDITIONS IN COLD CLIMATES

In simple terms, there are two types of cold to worry about. The first type is dry cold. Although this is very often accompanied by lower temperatures, it is easier to cope with in terms of clothing and equipment. Secondly, there is wet cold, which is more of a problem because of rain, sleet, snow and ice. Becoming cold and wet can be extremely dangerous.

BEFORE

Equipment

Survival pack

This should contain:

- tent
- sleeping bag
- stove and fuel
- food and drink
- matches
- rope
- map and compass
- whistle, torch and spare battery
- spare items of clothing

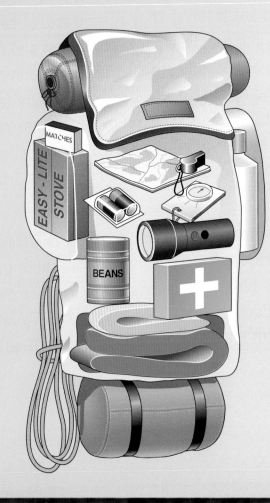

Tents

Your tent needs to be robust, double-skinned, and easily and quickly put up. It must provide a porch and have a sewn-in groundsheet. Make sure that you can pitch your tent in the most difficult conditions, so practise beforehand in the garden.

Sleeping bags

Buy the best one you can afford. It will be light and non-bulky to carry and will keep you warm in the coldest temperatures.

Stoves

Make sure that the fuel your stove uses is available in the country you are visiting.

Clothing

Check that your coat and overtrousers are water and wind proof. Make sure that the coat is loosely cut with plenty of room to move your arms and allow for extra layers of clothing underneath. Hats and gloves or mitts are essential. Your hands and feet are furthest from your heart and will get cold first.

Food
Expedition rations must be light in weight: (maximum 1 kg per person per day) and small in bulk (you may need to carry up to seven days' rations in your rucksack). The food must be easy and quick to prepare, appetizing and provide adequate nutrition and calories.

Tents
Do not cook inside a tent. Use the porch instead.

Sleeping bags
Make sure your sleeping bag never gets wet. In extreme cases it will be the only thing that can keep you alive.

Clothing
One or more spare pairs of gloves should be carried by every member of the group in case someone drops theirs or they are blown away.

Frozen hands are uncomfortable and in extreme cold, bare flesh will freeze to metal. Boots must have thick soles and leather uppers to keep your feet warm.

Food
You need plenty of calories for trekking, climbing, etc. but you will also use up calories just keeping warm. You should have at least 4000 kilocalories per person per day and ideally more.

The ascent of Everest

Mountain experts

An interview with Sir Edmund Hillary

Questions	Answers
How did you have enough energy to climb Mount Everest?	I was very fit and had much climbing experience.
How do other mountains you've climbed compare to Everest? Can you think of another peak that's challenged you as much as Everest?	Other mountains have more technically difficult routes than Everest. But none have that last 800 feet (300 m) of extreme height.
How did you sleep on Mount Everest?	Sleeping is always difficult at high altitude, so we didn't sleep much.
Did you have to carry all your own food, or was there some food available on the mountain, such as plants? How much food did you take? What kind of food did you eat?	We carried all our own food. High on the mountain, food is repugnant and you have to make yourself eat. Most of our energy came from very sweet drinks – mostly hot weak tea with lots of sugar.
Was there a time up on Everest when you were scared? Can you describe what was happening?	I was scared many times on Everest, but this is all part of the challenge. When I fell down a crevasse it was pretty scary.
How long did it take you to climb Mount Everest?	It took seven weeks to go from base camp to the top, but only three days coming down.
How did you feel when you reached the top of Everest? Were you able to see anything? What did the world look like from up there?	On the summit of Everest I had a feeling of great satisfaction to be first there. We could see a vast distance in every direction – mostly mountains, glaciers, and high plateaux.
How does it feel to be called 'Sir'? What was it like being knighted?	Becoming 'Sir' is slightly uncomfortable at first although it is a considerable honour. It is amazing how quickly you become accustomed to it. I still have the same friends and a similar way of life. The actual knighting took place in Buckingham Palace by the Queen – it was a very impressive ceremony.

George Mallory

George Leigh Mallory was born in 1886. Mallory was a schoolmaster but during the First World War he served at the front as a gunner. He was married with three children.

In 1924 a British expedition set out to climb Everest. At that time, no climber had been above 8000 m. It wasn't clear whether climbers could go higher and still survive, and whether oxygen would help.

George Mallory, then 38 years old, was one of Britain's best rock climbers, and he had already proved his fitness on expeditions to Everest in 1921 and 1922. His companion was a scientist called Andrew 'Sandy' Irvine, aged 22. Sandy had no high-altitude climbing experience. However, he was extremely good at repairing the oxygen bottles. The local Tibetans and Sherpas laughed at the bottles. They said they contained 'English air'.

On the morning of 6 June 1924, Mallory and Irvine had a breakfast of fried tinned sardines and set off from their camp at 7667 m. They planned to reach the summit three days later. On the way, they passed another climber, Howard Somervell, who lent his camera to Mallory so that he could take photographs if he reached the top.

Mallory and Irvine were last seen on 8 June by a geologist, Noel Odell, who was following behind. He saw two figures climbing a rock step on Everest's skyline. As far as Odell was concerned, they were doing well, and he thought they would definitely reach the summit.

Climbers Morehead, Mallory and Somervell – Everest expedition 1922

Odell went back to the camp but stayed up all night watching for signs of Mallory and Irvine's return. No one came back. Eventually the expedition was forced to accept the sad fact that Mallory and Irvine were lost on the mountain and probably dead.

For years afterwards, other climbers searched for Mallory and Irvine's bodies on Everest but no one found them. Then, in May 1999, a search team called the Mallory and Irvine Research Team found Mallory's body. It had been very well preserved by the ice and snow. The team buried his body on Everest, as his family requested. Irvine's body has still not been found and nor has the camera. The mystery of whether Mallory and Irvine ever reached the summit of Mount Everest remains unsolved.

Tourism in the mountains — good

THE POSITIVE EFFECTS

- provides good source of **income**

- higher standard of living

- money enables farmers to continue to farm and to buy land

- money enables local people to build new houses and maintain existing houses

- allows local people to stay in the mountains instead of having to look for work in the cities

- traditional crafts, e.g. carpet weaving, are preserved because tourists buy them

- visiting tourists realize how important the mountain environment is so encourage preservation

- tourism provides need for better communication links, e.g. roads, tunnels. Communities feel less isolated and able to reach hospitals and schools more easily.

or bad?

THE NEGATIVE EFFECTS

- trees cut down to build hotels and other tourist buildings

- trees used as fuel in hotels and tourist-related buildings

- environment suffers from forests being cut down. Animals and plants are under threat and some are facing extinction.

- building ski runs means destroying large areas of forest

- cutting down trees increases threat of landslides, erosion and avalanches

- local languages threatened because local people need to communicate in other languages to talk to tourists

- shop items expensive

- litter a big problem. In 1990s 33 tonnes of litter were cleared from the base of Mount Everest.

- road building and tunnel building means more trees cut down and environment suffers

- pollution created by extra traffic

- farming skills lost as local people get jobs in tourist industry

- many mountains sacred to local people – tourism means that holy places visited by many thousands of people, upsetting for local people

Mountain manners

Walking and climbing in the mountains is great fun but remember to respect the environment you are enjoying. Here are some guidelines on how to behave in the mountains.

1 Conserve the mountain environment

No cairns

2 Respect local land use

KEEP YOUR DISTANCE !!

Avoid polluting the environment

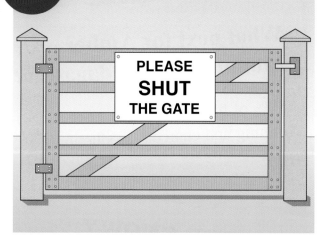

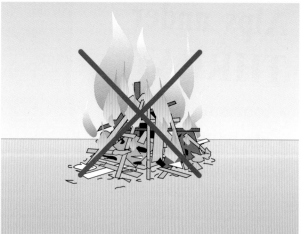

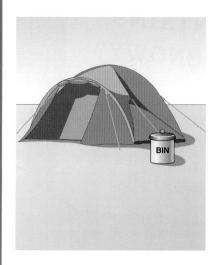

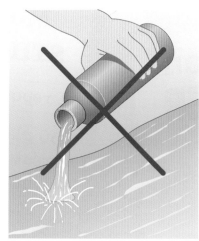

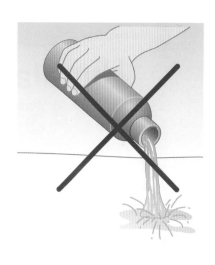

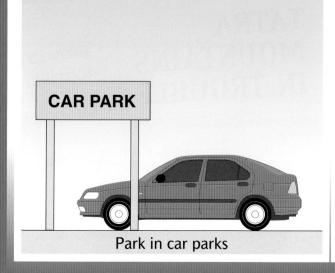

Park in car parks

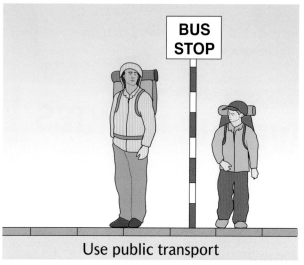

Use public transport

Saving the mountain

Alps under THREAT

- tourism
- air pollution
- traditional farming methods are being lost

What next for Amber Mountains in Madagascar?

80% of forests lost to farming, mining and charcoal production

Himalayan DISASTER

- war
- deforestation
- drought
- logging
- overgrazing
- poor treatment of mountain people

ARE THE SNOWY MOUNTAINS STILL SNOWY?

A report from Australia

250 plant species under threat from a series of warm winters

SAVE THE ROCKIES

- development, including recreational activities
- house building on prime land
- climate change

TATRA MOUNTAINS IN TROUBLE

A report from our eastern European correspondent

- growth in tourism
- air pollution

environment

Save the Hengduan Mountains in China
Rapidly developing tourism threatens mountain peoples' cultures

LOGGING CHAOS
in Sierra Chincua, Mexico
Logging and agricultural expansion have destroyed 44% of the forest

Ravages of war in Pamir Mountains, Tajikistan

Civil war has resulted in widespread poverty

> Maintaining our mountains in their natural state is essential to the well-being of us all, we mustn't let these mountains be ruined for ever.

The Great Smokey mountains go up in smoke

- air pollution

Glossary

altitude   the height of something above sea level

archipelago   a group of islands

avalanche   a fall or slide of snow or rock down a mountainside

blizzard   a very heavy snowstorm with high winds

broadleaf   trees with broad rather than needle-like leaves

cascade   to fall like a waterfall

cholera   deadly disease caused by drinking polluted water containing the cholera bacteria

coniferous   trees that are mostly needle-leaved, such as pines, spruces and firs

conservationist   someone who protects and takes care of the environment

debris   the scattered remains of something destroyed

deciduous   trees that lose their leaves at the end of the growing season

evergreen   trees that don't lose their leaves

fauna   a group of animals, especially the animals of a particular region

flora   a group of plants, especially the plants of a particular region

geologist   someone who studies the origin, history and structure of the Earth

geothermal energy   energy produced from hot springs

glacier   a mass of ice that slowly creeps down a snowy mountain

gorge   a deep narrow passage with steep, rocky sides

headwater   the source or highest part of a stream

income   the money people earn from working

itinerary   a journey plan

jaundice   an illness where skin turns yellow because the liver isn't working properly

magma   hot, molten rock that comes up from within the Earth to the Earth's surface, usually via a volcano

mantle   the layer of the Earth between the crust and the core

mineral   a rock that is mined because it is useful to humans

mining   digging out the useful mineral

pilgrim   someone who makes a special trip to go to a holy shrine or sacred place

plunder   to rob or steal

rainforest   a thick evergreen forest in a tropical region with an annual rainfall of at least 2.5 metres

range   a chain of mountains

spring   a small stream of water flowing naturally from within the Earth

subtropical   close to a tropical area and having an almost tropical climate

tribe   a group of people who share a common history and culture

vegetation   plants

vulcanologist   someone who studies volcanoes

wadi   a valley that remains dry except during the rainy season

watershed   the imaginary line on a mountain where water either flows down one side of the mountain or the other

western hemisphere   the half of the globe which includes North and South America

Bibliography

Books

Non-fiction

Chambers, C. *Mountains*
ISBN: 0 431 09845 X

Knapp, B. *The Mountain Book*
ISBN: 1 862140 28 6

Rogers, D. *Geography Starts Here: Volcanoes*
ISBN: 0 7502 4156 X

Sauvain, P. *Geography Detective: Mountains*
ISBN: 1 874488 592

Walker, J. *Natural Disasters: Avalanches and Landslides*
ISBN: 07496 4406 0

Fiction

Ransome, A. *Swallows and Amazons*
(plus other titles by the same author)
ISBN: 022460631X

Dillon, J. *Surviving – Snow Trap*
ISBN: 01 41 30445 6

Internet

http://www.bear-rescue.tv/

http://www.globaleye.org.uk/primary/focuson/index.html

http://www.mountains2002.org

http://www.bbc.co.uk/england/everest/world/hillary.shtml

http://www.metoffice.com

http://www.teacher.scholastic.com/hillary/bio

Organizations

WWF
Panda House
Weyside Park
Godalming
Surrey
GU7 1XR
http://www.panda.org

Scout Association
Gilwell Park
Bury Road
Chingford
London
E4 7QW
http://www.scouts.org.uk

British Tourist Authority
Thames Tower
Blacks Road
Hammersmith
London
W6 9EL
http://www.visitbritain.com

The Woodland Trust
Autumn Park
Grantham
Lincolnshire
NG31 6LL
www.woodland-trust.org.uk

Forestry Commission
231 Corstorphine Road
Edinburgh
Scotland
EH12 7AT
www.forestry.gov.uk

Index